NATURE WONDERLAND

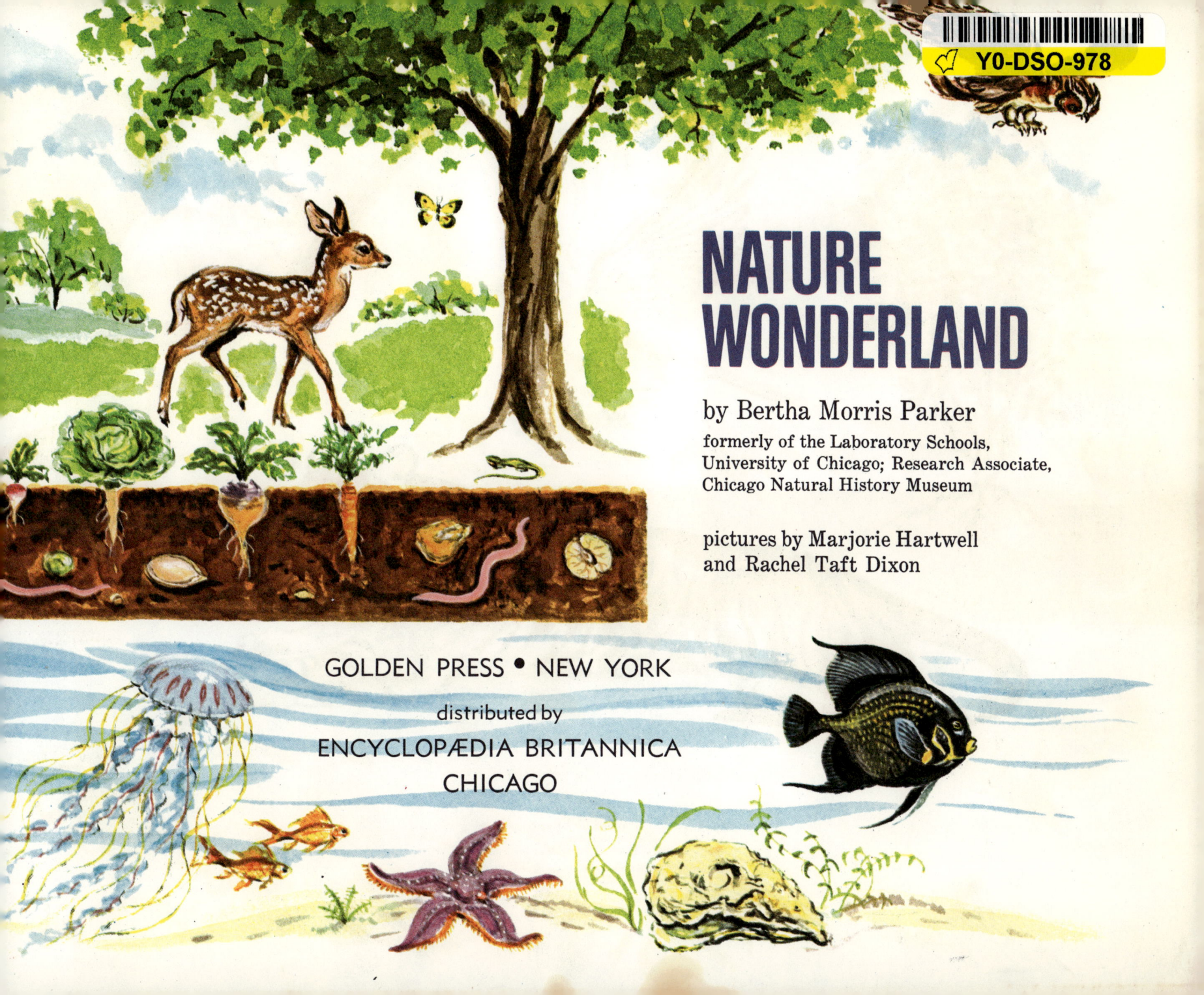

by Bertha Morris Parker
formerly of the Laboratory Schools,
University of Chicago; Research Associate,
Chicago Natural History Museum

pictures by Marjorie Hartwell
and Rachel Taft Dixon

GOLDEN PRESS • NEW YORK

distributed by
ENCYCLOPÆDIA BRITANNICA
CHICAGO

rose

bluebird

squirrel

tiger

1970 EDITION

© Copyright 1963 by Western Publishing Company, Inc.
All rights reserved.
Printed in the U.S.A. by Western Publishing Company, Inc.
Library of Congress Catalog Card Number: 63-17546.

monarch caterpillar

milkweed

All these are alive.

Find two animals with fur.

Find two animals with feathers.

Find two plants with flowers.

Find an animal on a plant.

morning glory

peacock

5

One of these is alive.

Which one?

submarine

blue whale

hummingbird

weather balloon

kite

helicopter

barn swallows

Which of these are alive?

7

Living things grow.

This little snail

may grow to be as big as this.

This little violet plant

may grow to be as big as this.

Will this toy clown

ever grow to be any bigger?

Which ones will never grow
to be any bigger?

Here are some animals.
Can you find
    a brown cow,
    a pink pig,
    a white goat,
    a black bear,
    an orange goldfish,
    a yellow duckling,
    a gray toad,
    a green turtle,
    a blue butterfly,
    and a purple starfish?

Find two cows.

Find three bears.

What are all the other animals?

Ten of these animals are dogs.

The other one is a wild relative.

Can you find it?

Do you know what it is?

poodle

collie

Dalmatian

beagle

dachshund

Boston terrier

Pomeranian

cocker spaniel

Old English sheepdog

German shepherd

fox

Ten legs,
    eight legs,
        six legs,
            four legs,
        two legs,
            no legs.
Which animal has which?

lobster

katydid

squirrel

daddy longlegs

ostrich

earthworm

One yellow butterfly,
   two green grasshoppers,
   three fuzzy bumblebees,
   four spotted ladybugs,
   five little red ants.
And every one has six legs.
Count their legs.
These are all insects.
All insects have six legs.

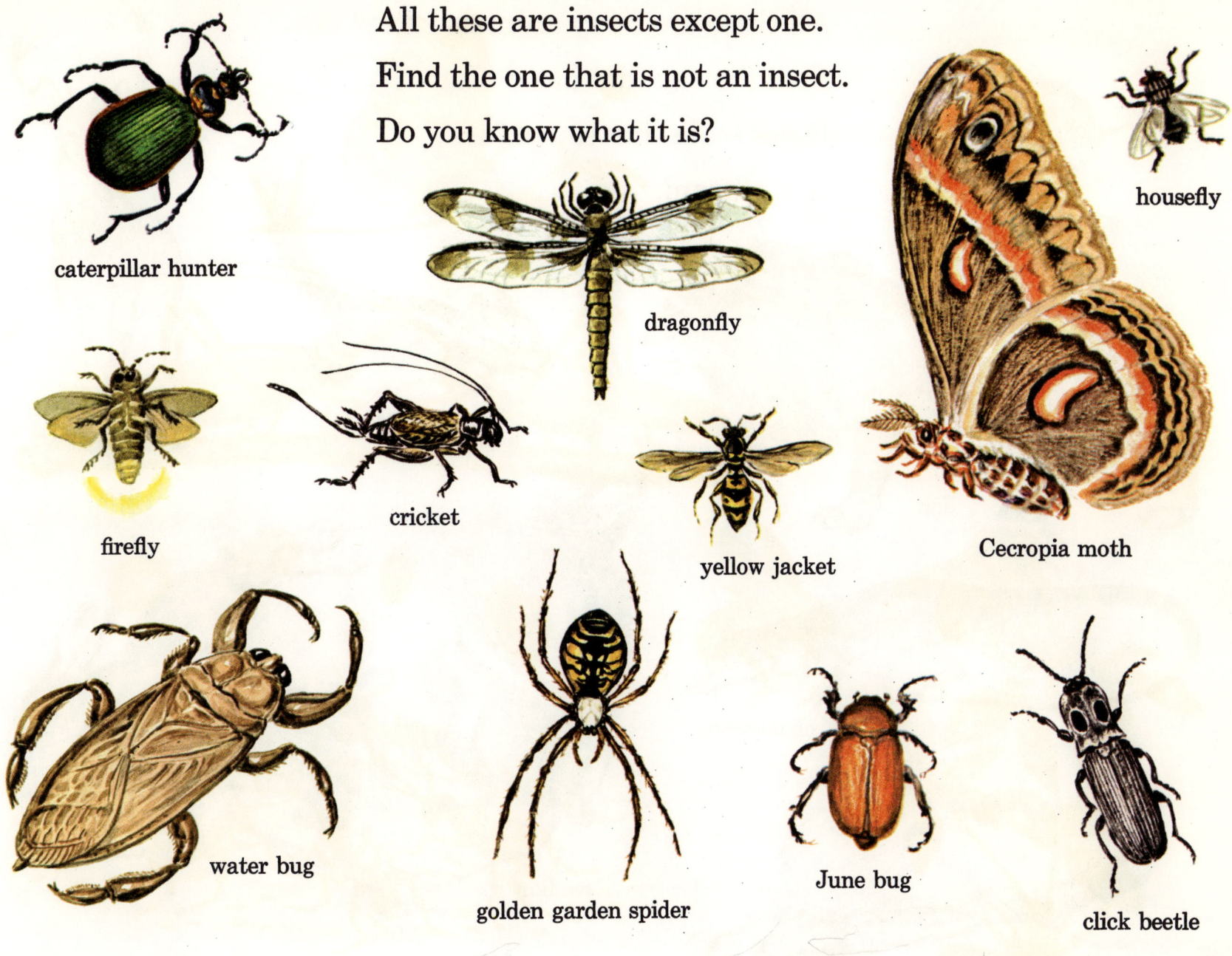

All these are insects except one.
Find the one that is not an insect.
Do you know what it is?

caterpillar hunter

dragonfly

housefly

firefly

cricket

yellow jacket

Cecropia moth

water bug

golden garden spider

June bug

click beetle

15

All these are furry animals except one.
Find the one that has no fur.
It has scales instead of fur.
It is a lizard.

mouse

lion

chipmunk

deer

chameleon

sea lion

cottontail

opossum

16

chickadee

blue jay

parrot

bat

woodpecker

pigeon

meadowlark

goldfinch

pelican

duck

All these animals can fly.
All of them are birds except one.
Find the one that is not a bird.
It has fur instead of feathers.

All these are toads or frogs except one.

The one that is not a toad or frog has a shell.

It has scales, too.

Find it.

Do you know what it is?

wood frog

tree toad

painted turtle

bullfrog

leopard frog

Fowler's toad

spring peeper

All these animals have shells.
All of them are turtles except one.
It does not have scales.
Find it.
What is it?

spotted turtle

box turtle

gopher tortoise

common snapper

diamondback

snail

slider

19

jellyfish

sailfish

whitefish

All these animals have fish in their names.

But one is not a real fish.

Find it.

How can you tell it is not a fish?

catfish

goldfish

angelfish

swordfish

sunfish

A giraffe makes almost no sound at all.
A bullfrog croaks.
"Jug-o-rum, jug-o-rum,"
   it seems to say. 
A crow caws.
A cow moos.
An elephant trumpets.
How many other animal sounds
   do you know?

Many animals that live in the sea have shells.

One of these animals has a shell
 that is all in one piece.

The other has a shell that closes
 like a pocketbook.

Which is which?

queen conch

clam

These are all seashells.
Find all those that close up
like a pocketbook.

lightning shell

top shell

screw shell

bleeding tooth

angel wing

star shell

kitten's paw

rock shell

old maid's curl

cockle

scallop

slipper shell

butterfly shell

turkey wing

Here is a hollyhock plant.

Find its stem.

Find a leaf.

Find a flower.

Find a root.

Here is a sunflower.

Find its stem.

Find a leaf and a flower.

It has roots, but where are they?

All vegetables come from plants.
Some vegetables are roots.
Some vegetables are leaves.
Which of these are roots?
Which are leaves?

radish

cabbage

spinach

beet

carrot

sweet potato

lettuce

turnip

Some of our vegetables are seeds.

Some are the parts of a plant that have seeds inside.

Find the vegetables that are seeds.

Find the vegetables that have seeds inside.

squash

green pepper

beans

peas

tomato

cucumber

All fruits come from plants.

Here are some fruits.

Can you name them all?

Trees are plants.
Do any of these trees
grow near your house?

elm

apple

maple

palm

oak

pine

maple willow pine apple

spruce elm oak fir

Here are eight trees in the winter.
Which ones would make good Christmas trees?

Here are some rows of tree leaves.

In each row one leaf is different.

Find the leaves that are different.

The different leaf is a cottonwood.

The different leaf is a willow.

The different leaf is a buckeye.

pussy willow

Bushes are plants.
Do any of these bushes
grow near your house?

snowball

snowberry

rose

bridal wreath

lilac

elderberry

red haw

31

Vines are plants.

Three of these vines have pretty flowers.

Find them.

Two have fruit that is good to eat.

Find them.

Do you know the other one?

grapevine

trumpet vine

climbing rose

honeysuckle

ivy

watermelon

Garden flowers are plants.
Find the tulip and the crocus.
They bloom in the spring.
Find the chrysanthemum.
It blooms in the fall.
The other flowers bloom in the summer.

tiger lily

daisy

petunia

nasturtium

poppy

pansy

tulip

marigold

crocus

chrysanthemum

four-o'clock

33

In each row there are three pictures of a wild flower and one of a garden flower.

The wild flowers are violets, wild roses, and buttercups.

Find the garden flower in each row and tell its name.

begonia

African violet

geranium

daffodil

foliage plant

tulip

These plants will grow in pots indoors.
Do you have any of them in your house?
Which one do you like best?

These animals live in water.

The one with ten legs
   is a crayfish.

The one with flippers
   is a dolphin.

The one with a shell like a pocketbook
   is an oyster.

The one that looks like a flower
   is a sea anemone.

What are the others?

36

These plants live in water.

Some are cattails.

Some are water lilies.

Their names tell which are which.

These animals spend most of their time in the air.

Find the one that is furry.

Find the one that has feathers.

What are the others?

The plant with the beautiful flowers is an orchid.

Where is it growing?

The long gray strands are long moss.

Where are they growing?

See how a butterfly grows up.
Does the baby butterfly look
like the grown-up butterfly?

egg

caterpillar

chrysalis

monarch butterfly

See how a bullfrog grows up.
Does the baby bullfrog look
like the grown-up bullfrog?

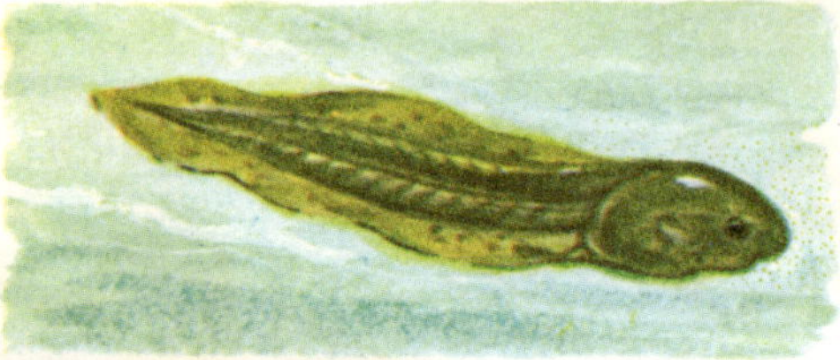

bullfrog

egg

tadpole

See how a robin grows up.
Does the baby robin look
   like the grown-up robin?

See how a kitten grows up.
Does the kitten change much
   as it grows up?

One of these baby animals is hatched from an egg.
Find it.
All the others are born.

What is happening here?

raccoon

What is happening here?

alligator

Here are four babies.

Find their mothers.

44

Here are four mothers.

Find their babies.

45

This big hippopotamus has a baby
that weighs twice as much as you do.

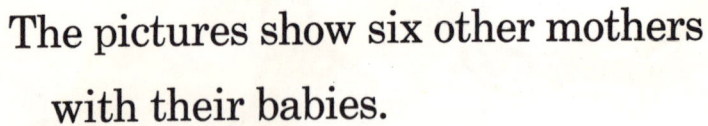

The pictures show six other mothers
with their babies.
The mother with one baby
is a koala.
The one with two babies
is a beaver.
The one with three babies
is a screech owl.

46

The one with four babies
   is an armadillo.
The one with half a dozen babies
   is a skunk.
The one with a dozen babies
   is a bobwhite.

47

See how a four-o'clock plant grows up.

See how a pumpkin vine grows up.

milkweed
radish
apple
wafer ash
sunflower
clematis
watermelon
catalpa
dandelion
peach
petunia
beggar-ticks
sweet pea
walnut
peanut
marigold
hollyhock
bean
lettuce
cedar
poppy
pine
nasturtium
coconut
grapefruit
These are all seeds.
Find the biggest seed
in the picture.
pumpkin
Find the tiniest seed.
morning glory

49

These seeds are getting rides
to new places to grow.
Find one that is getting
a ride on a puppy.
Find one that is being blown
by the wind.
The cherry the bird is carrying
has a seed inside it.

What is happening here?

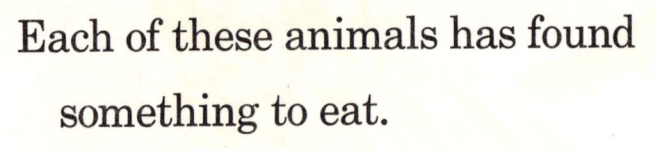

Each of these animals has found something to eat.

Which one has found a fish?

Which one has found an insect?

Which one has found some cabbage?

Which one has found a worm?

Which one has found some seeds?

What is happening here?

What is happening here?

scarlet tanager

fox squirrel

What has happened here?

A barnacle like this one

settles down on a rock

and stays there the rest of its life.

But most animals move about.

Look at the pictures.

Find an animal hopping.

Find one swimming.

Find one flying.

Find one climbing.

Find one running.

Find one walking.

Find one crawling.

Find one swinging along by its arms.

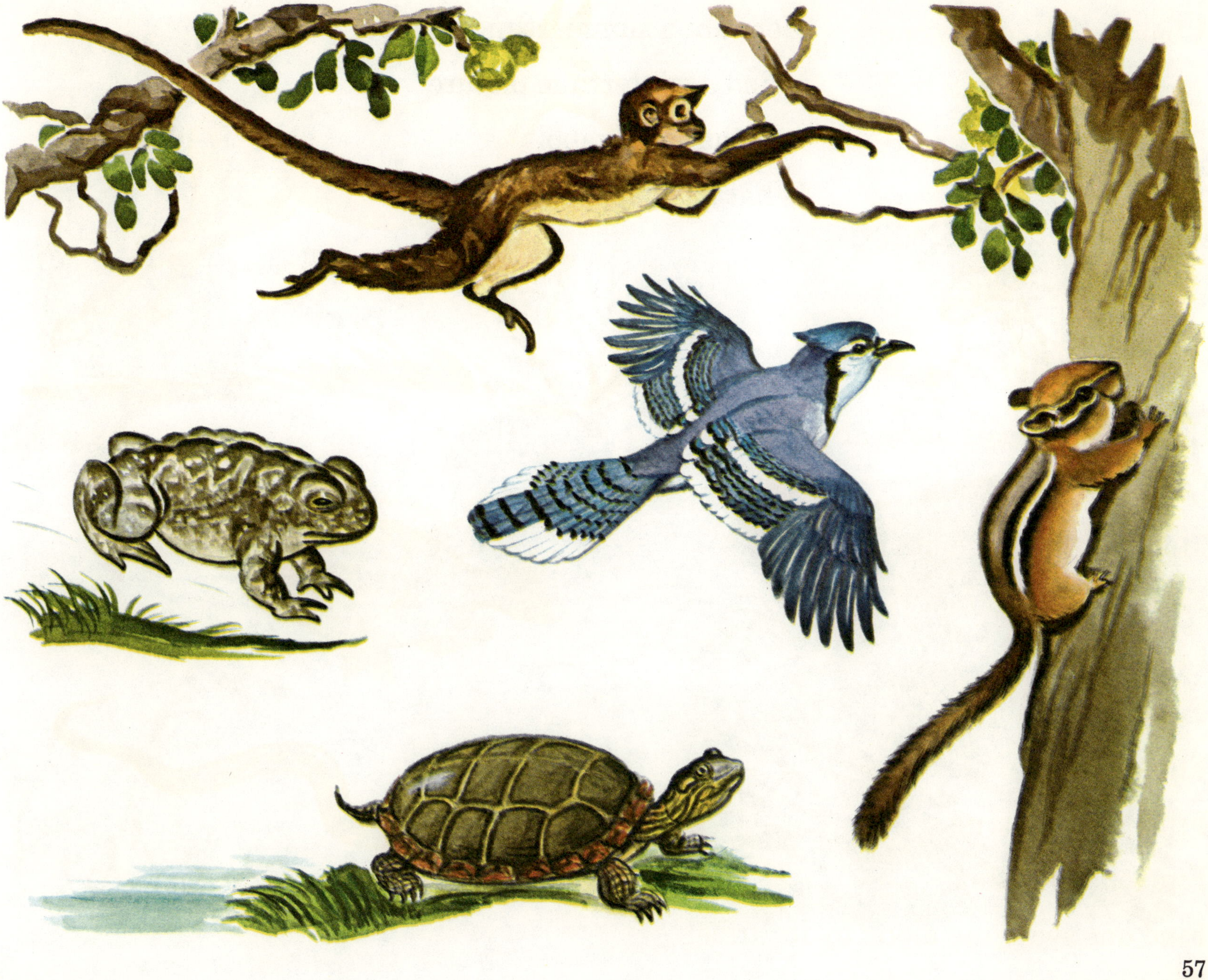

Here are a summertime picture
and a wintertime picture
of the same rabbit.
What has happened?

It is winter.

What signs of winter do you see?

It is spring.

What signs of spring do you see?

It is summer.

What signs of summer do you see?

61

It is fall.

What signs of fall do you see?